In this workbook, you'll be on your way to master reading and writing music notes, rhythm and more! We'll learn to write on the staff, and find the correct notes so we can create, read, and perform music. We'll dive into the world of note names and discover what those musical symbols are. And we're going to learn music rhythms and music bars with answers and a bonus part at the end. This is the <u>official supplement book</u> to <u>Essential Music Theory for Kids and Beginners Book #1 & Book #2</u> by Livingcolors Publishing.

Music is a powerful tool for self-expression and emotional well-being. It allows children to explore and express their feelings, whether it's joy, sadness, or excitement. It nurtures their confidence and self-esteem, as they discover their unique voices and talents. Music also brings people together, fostering teamwork, empathy, and a sense of belonging. Through music, we can build lifelong skills and create memories that will last a lifetime.

Just For You!

A FREE GIFT TO OUR READERS

Fun coloring book
pages from some of our
favorite books! Go online to

livingcolorspublishing.com

See the corresponding notes on the keyboard below

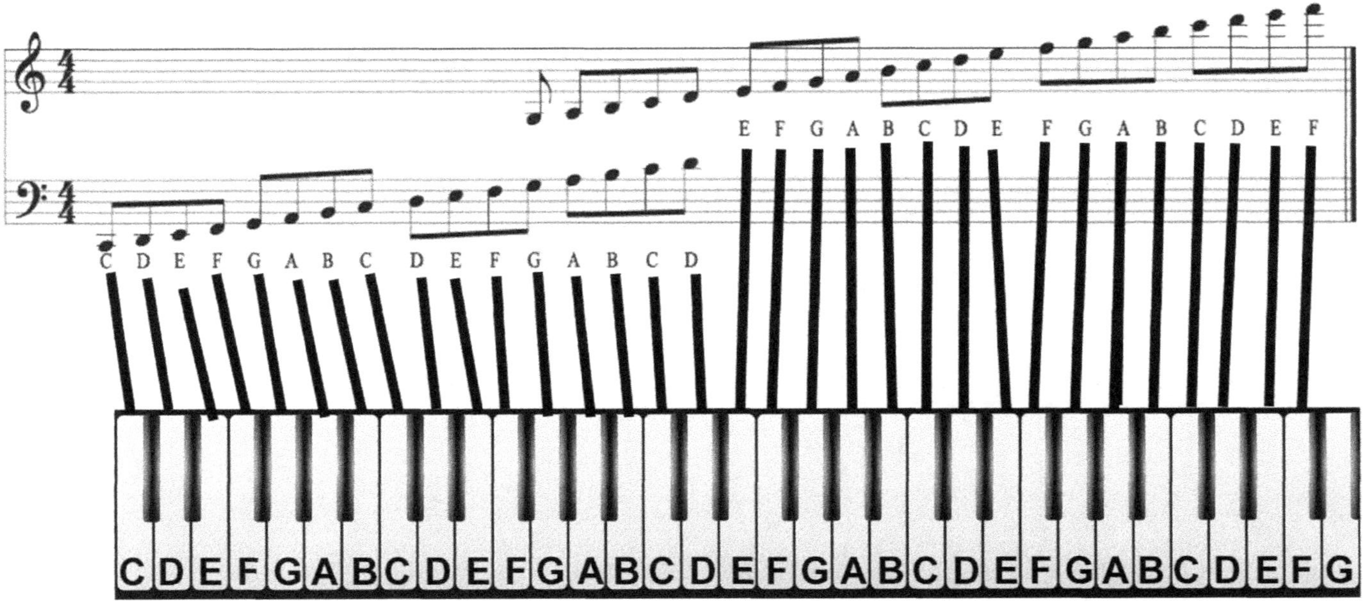

E F G A B C D E F G A B C D E F
C D E F G A B C D E F G A B C D
C D E F G A B C D E F G A B C D E F G A B C D E F G A B C D E F G

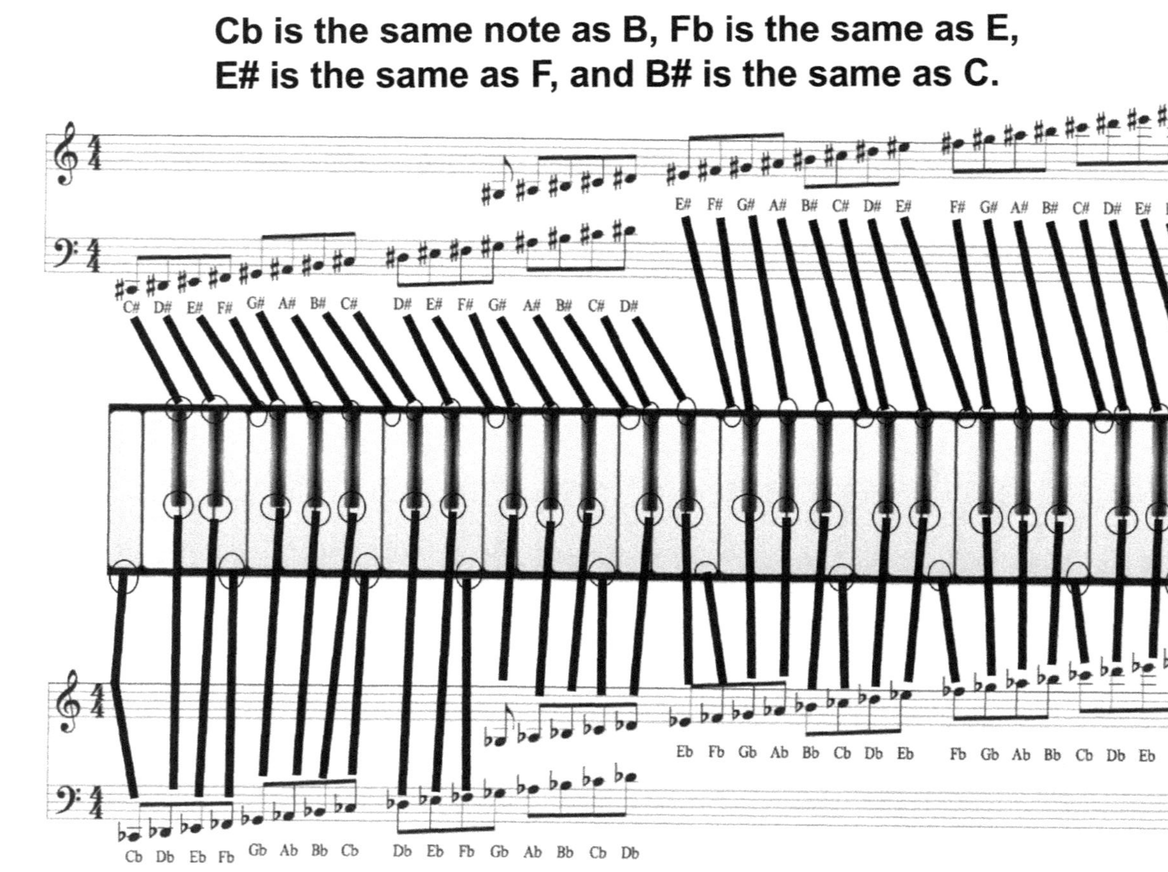
Cb is the same note as B, Fb is the same as E,
E# is the same as F, and B# is the same as C.
C# D# E# F# G# A# B# C# D# E# F# G# A# B# C# D#
E# F# G# A# B# C# D# E# F# G# A# B# C# D# E# F#
Cb Db Eb Fb Gb Ab Bb Cb Db Eb Fb Gb Ab Bb Cb Db
Eb Fb Gb Ab Bb Cb Db Eb Fb Gb Ab Bb Cb Db Eb Fb

NOTE NAMES ON TREBLE AND BASS CLEF

MIDDLE C ON A PIANO KEYBOARD IS C4

NOTE NAMES ON KEYBOARD & SHARPS AND FLATS

SHARP WRITTEN NEXT TO THE NOTE NAME RAISES THE NOTE BY HALF STEP

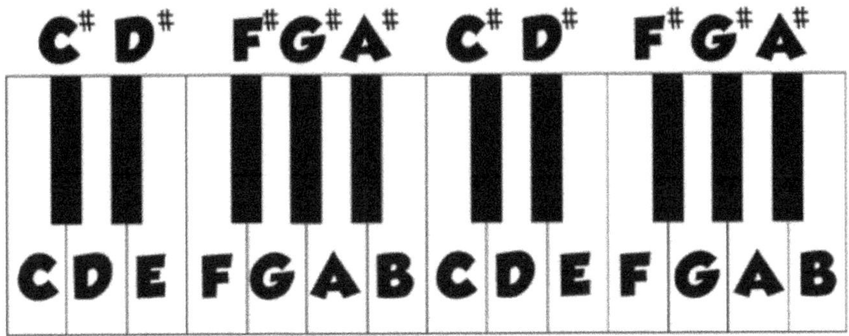

FLAT WRITTEN NEXT TO THE NOTE NAME LOWERS THE NOTE BY HALF STEP

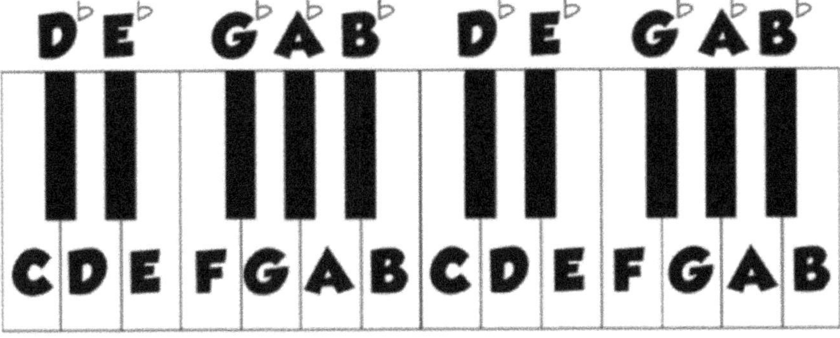

WRITE THE NOTE NAMES
ABOVE THE LINES

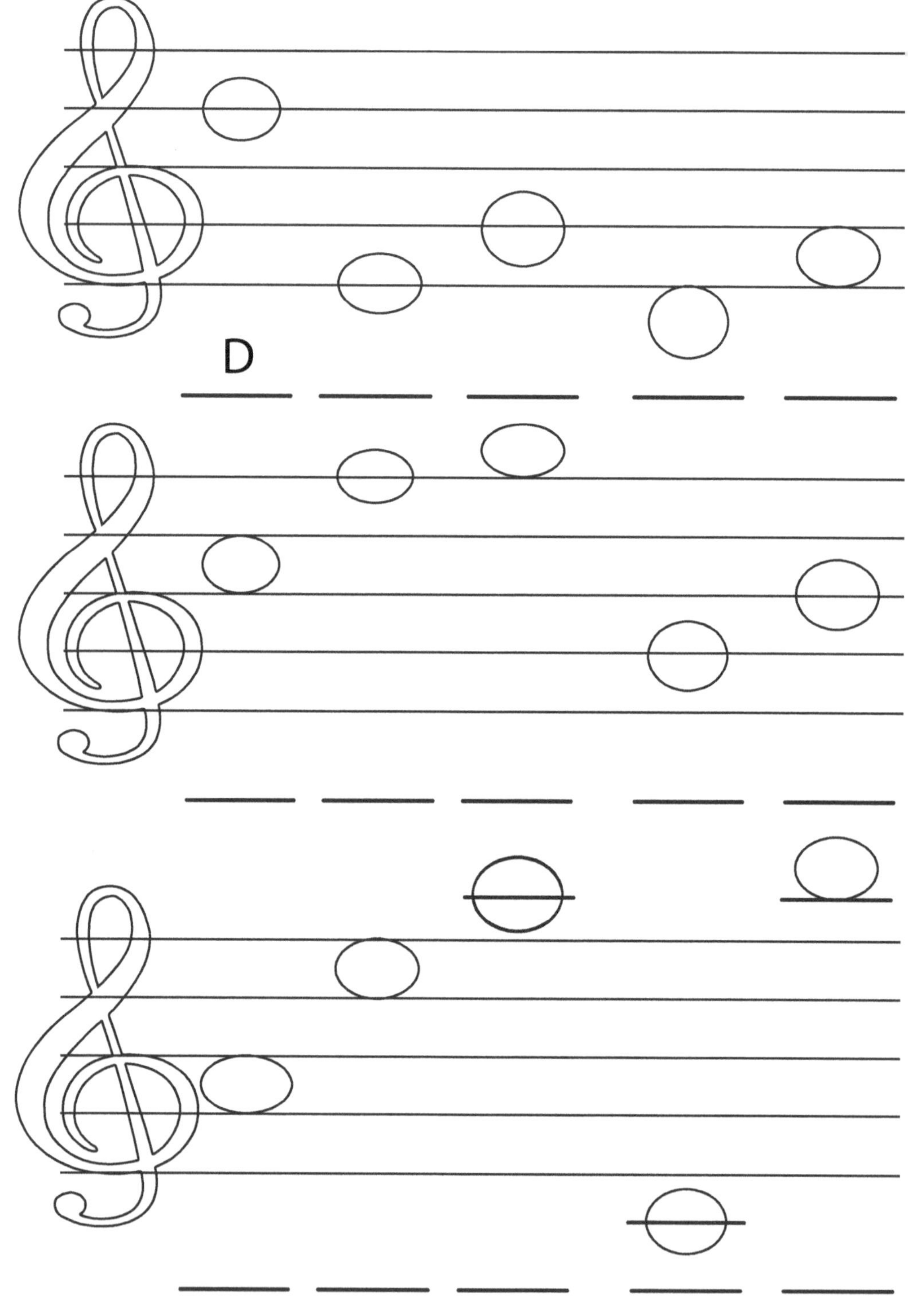

WRITE THE MUSIC NOTES

WRITE THE MUSIC NOTES

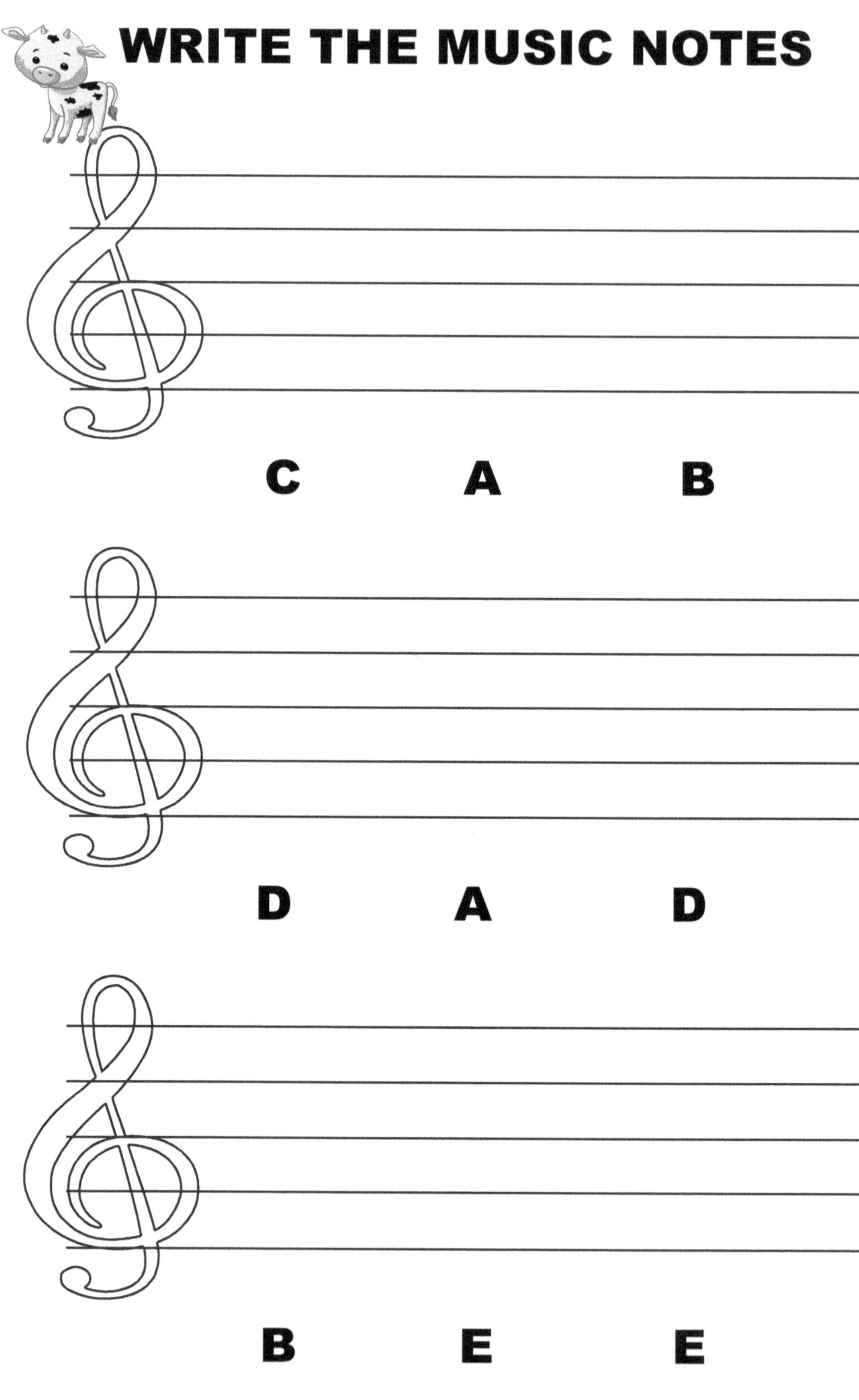

WRITE THE MUSIC NOTES

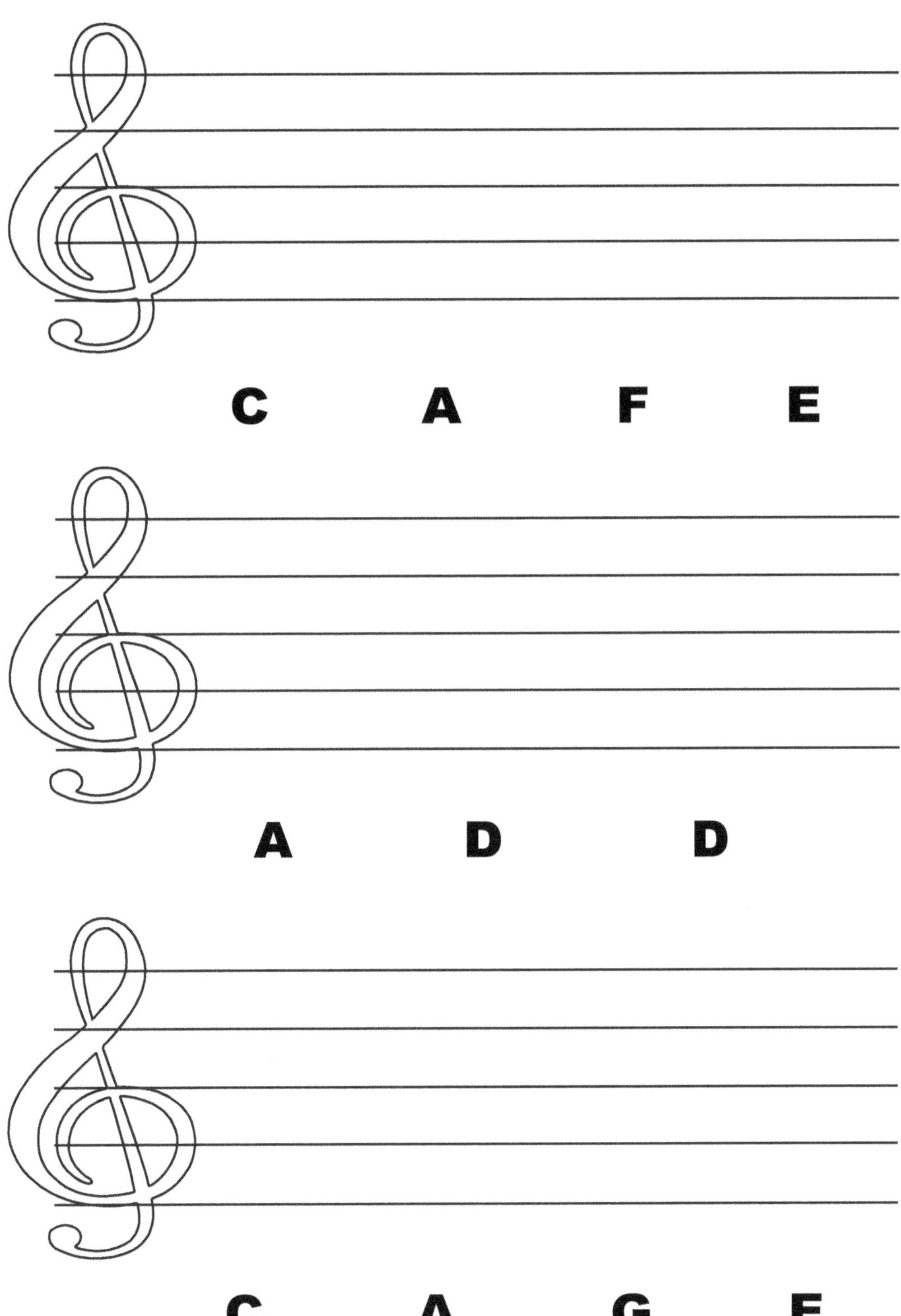

WRITE THE MUSIC NOTES

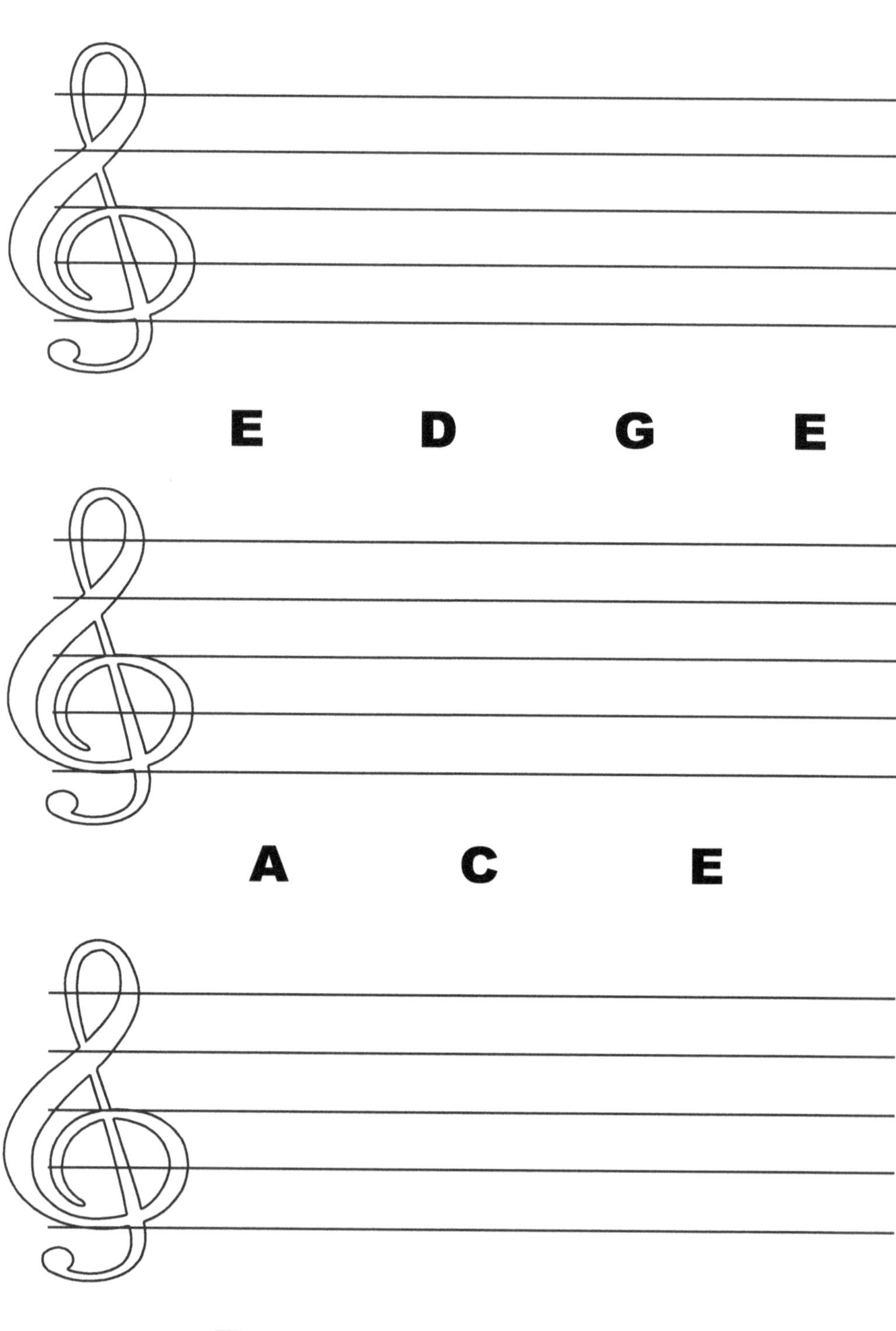

WRITE THE MUSIC NOTES

WRITE THE MUSIC NOTES

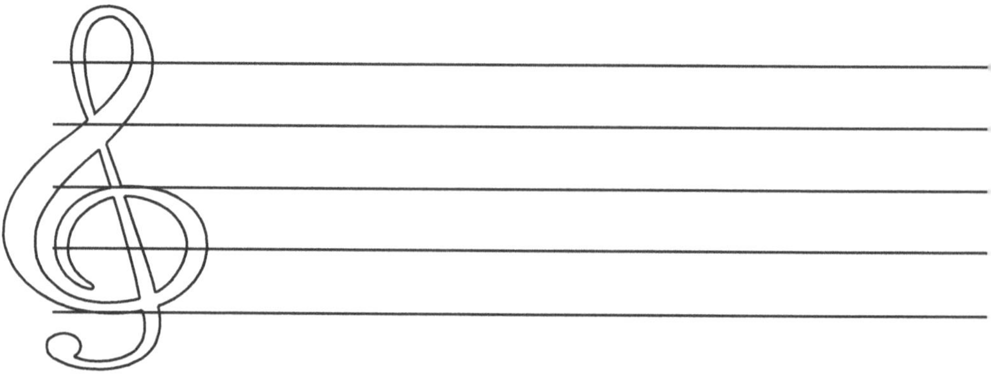

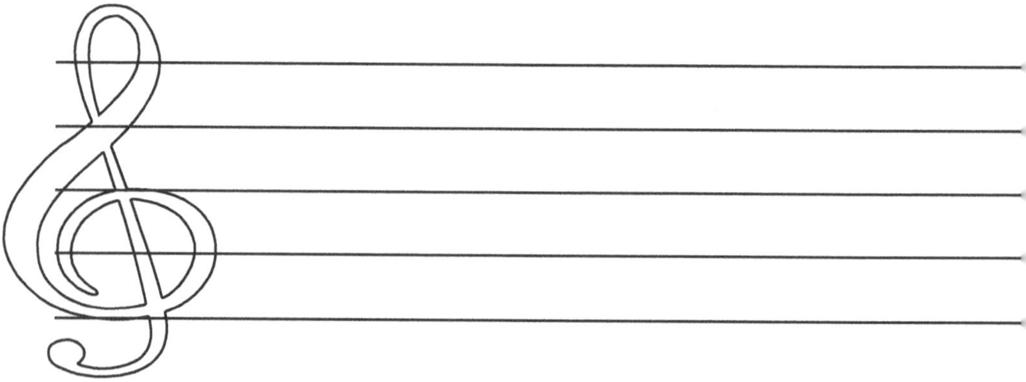

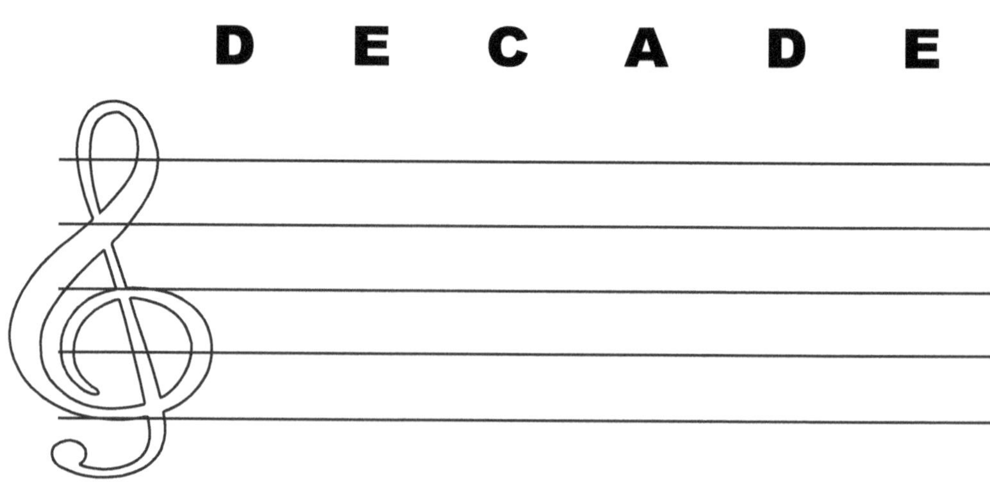

WRITE THE MUSIC NOTES

WRITE THE NOTE NAMES
ABOVE THE LINES

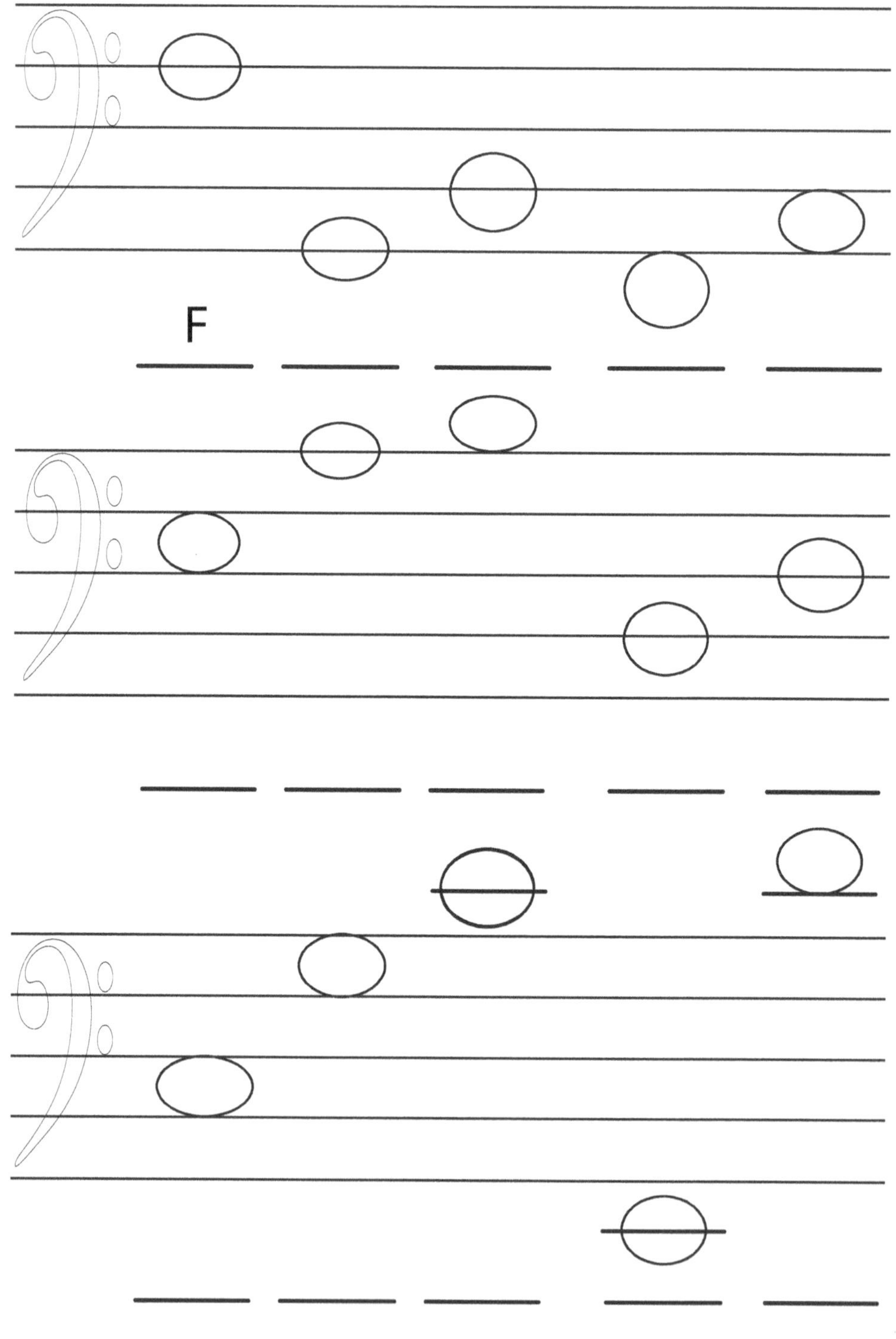

WRITE THE MUSIC NOTES

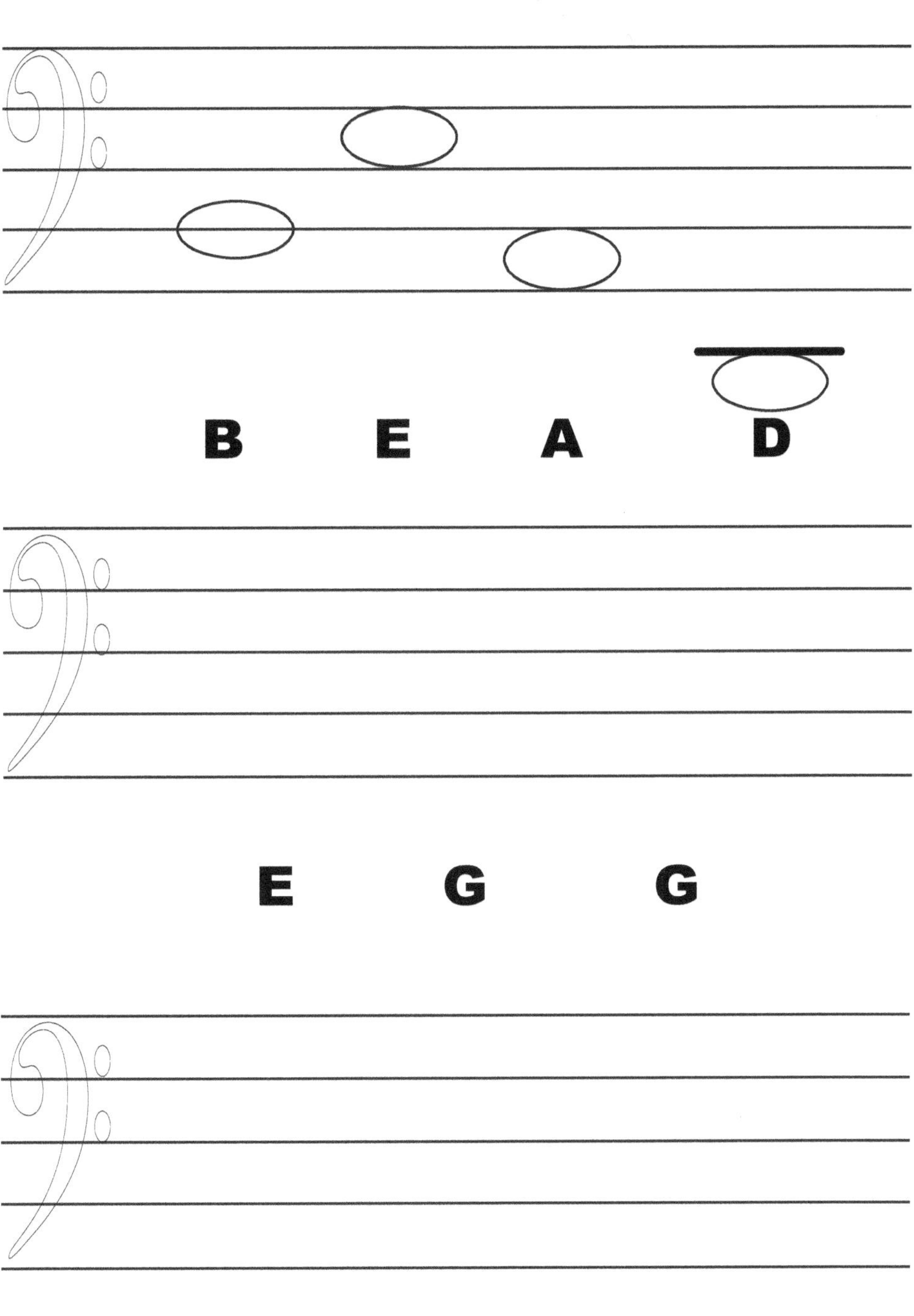

WRITE THE MUSIC NOTES

C   A   B

D   A   D

B   E   E

WRITE THE MUSIC NOTES

C A F E

A D D

C A G E

WRITE THE MUSIC NOTES

E   D   G   E

A   C   E

F   A   D   E

WRITE THE MUSIC NOTES

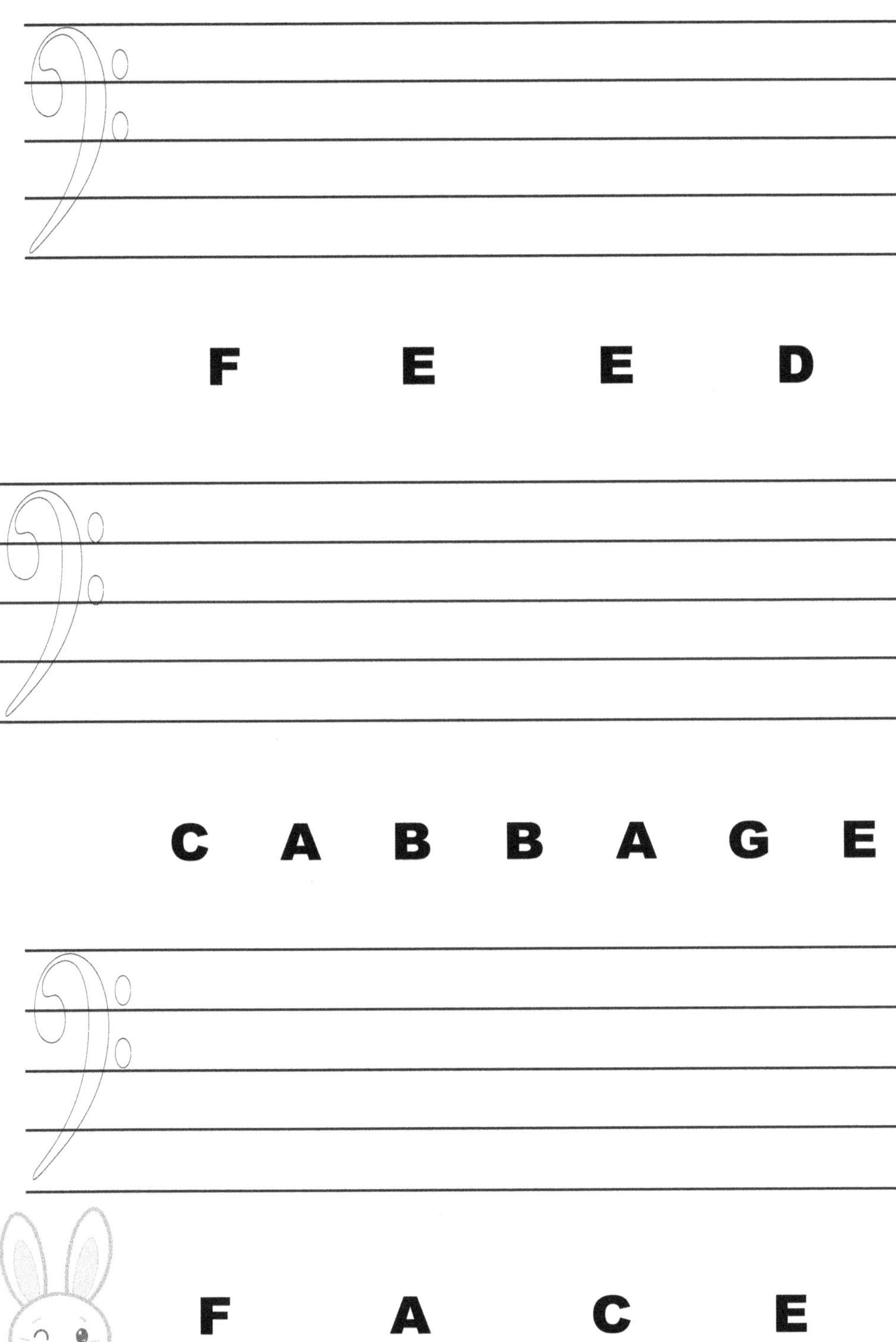

WRITE THE MUSIC NOTES

B   E   E   F

D   E   C   A   D   E

A   B   B   A

WRITE THE MUSIC NOTES

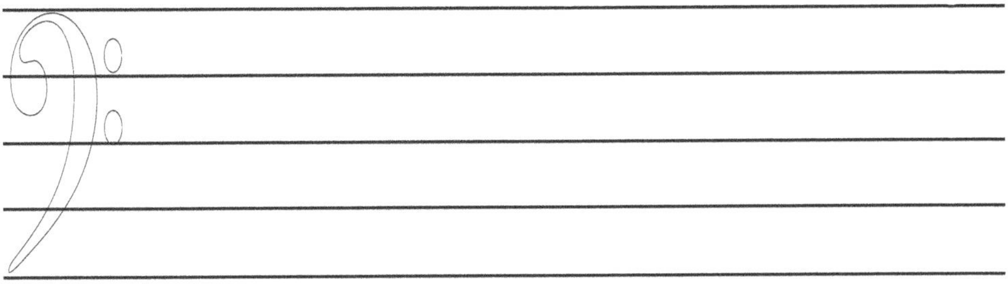

A   G   E

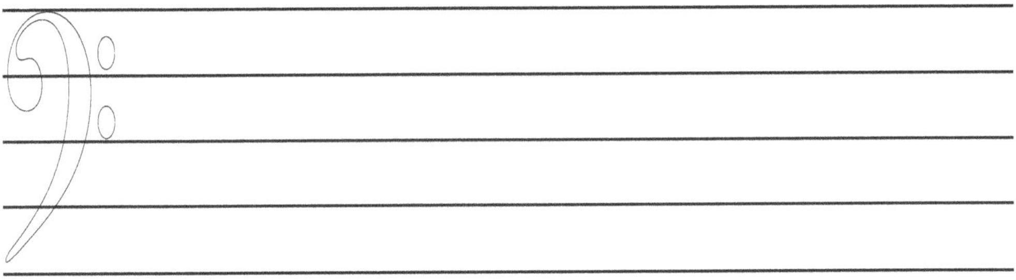

B   E   D

WRITE THE NOTE NAMES ABOVE THE LINES

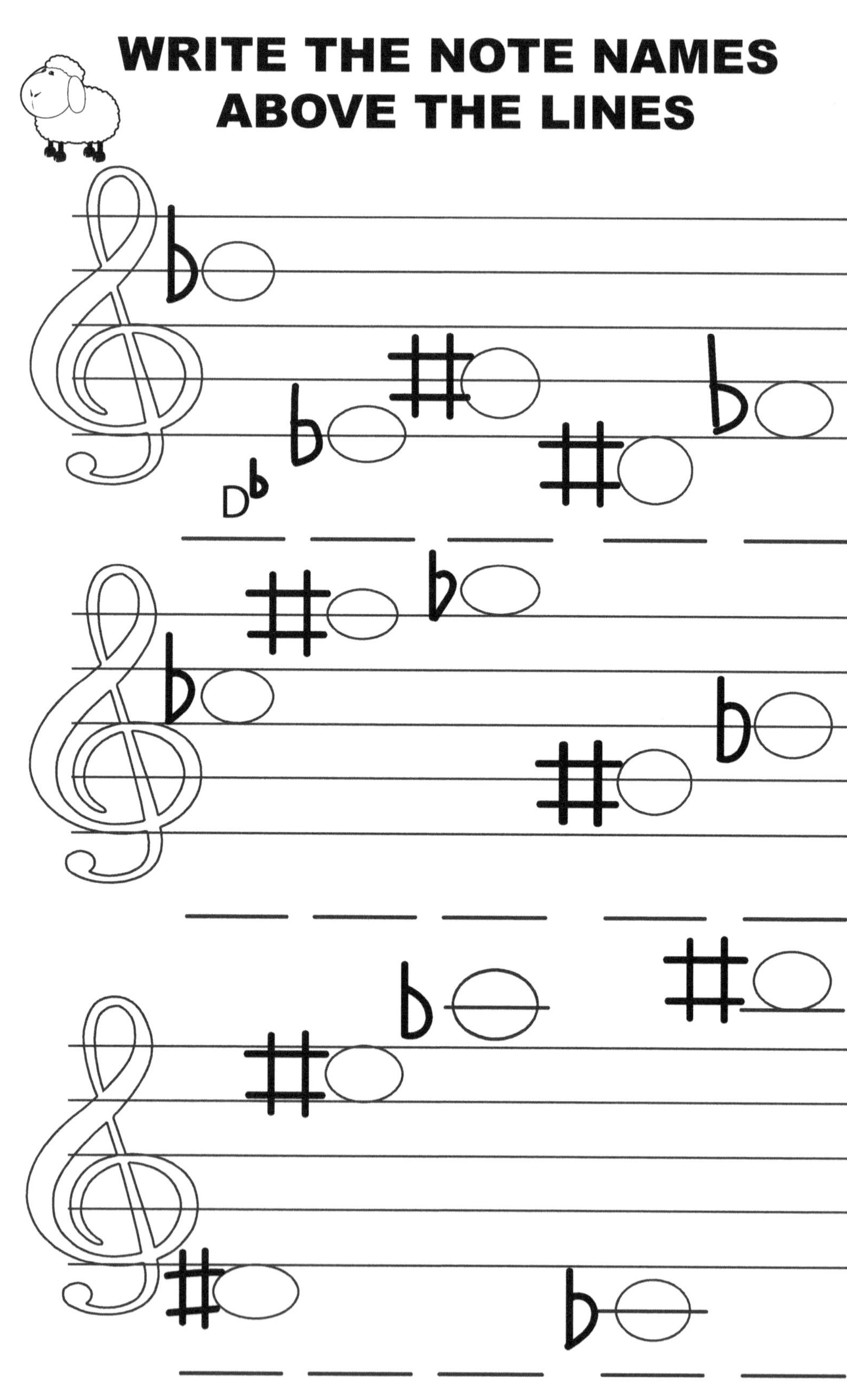

WRITE THE NOTE NAMES
ABOVE THE LINES

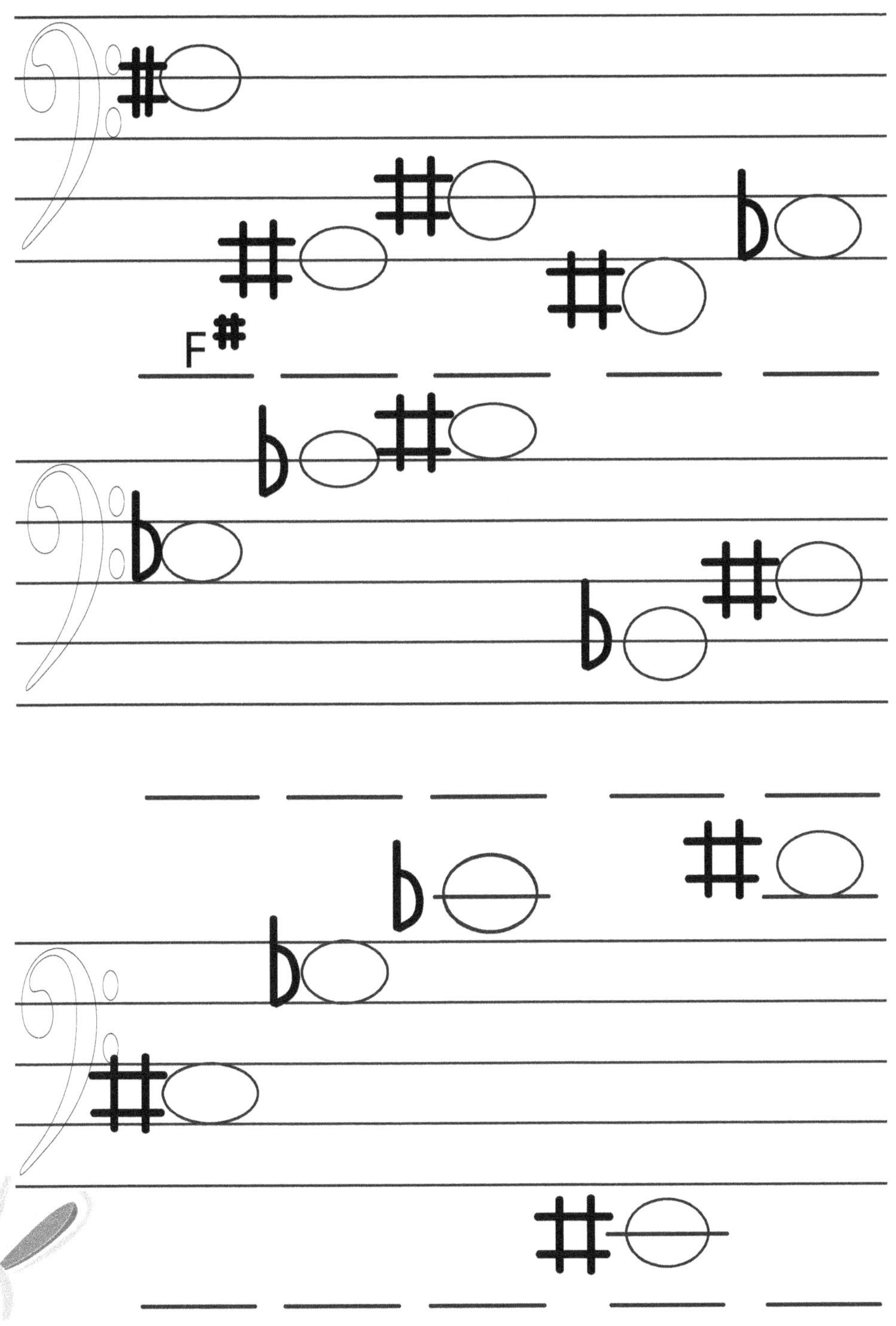

DRAW THE CORRECT CLEF ON STAFF
IS IT BASS CLEF OR TREBLE CLEF?

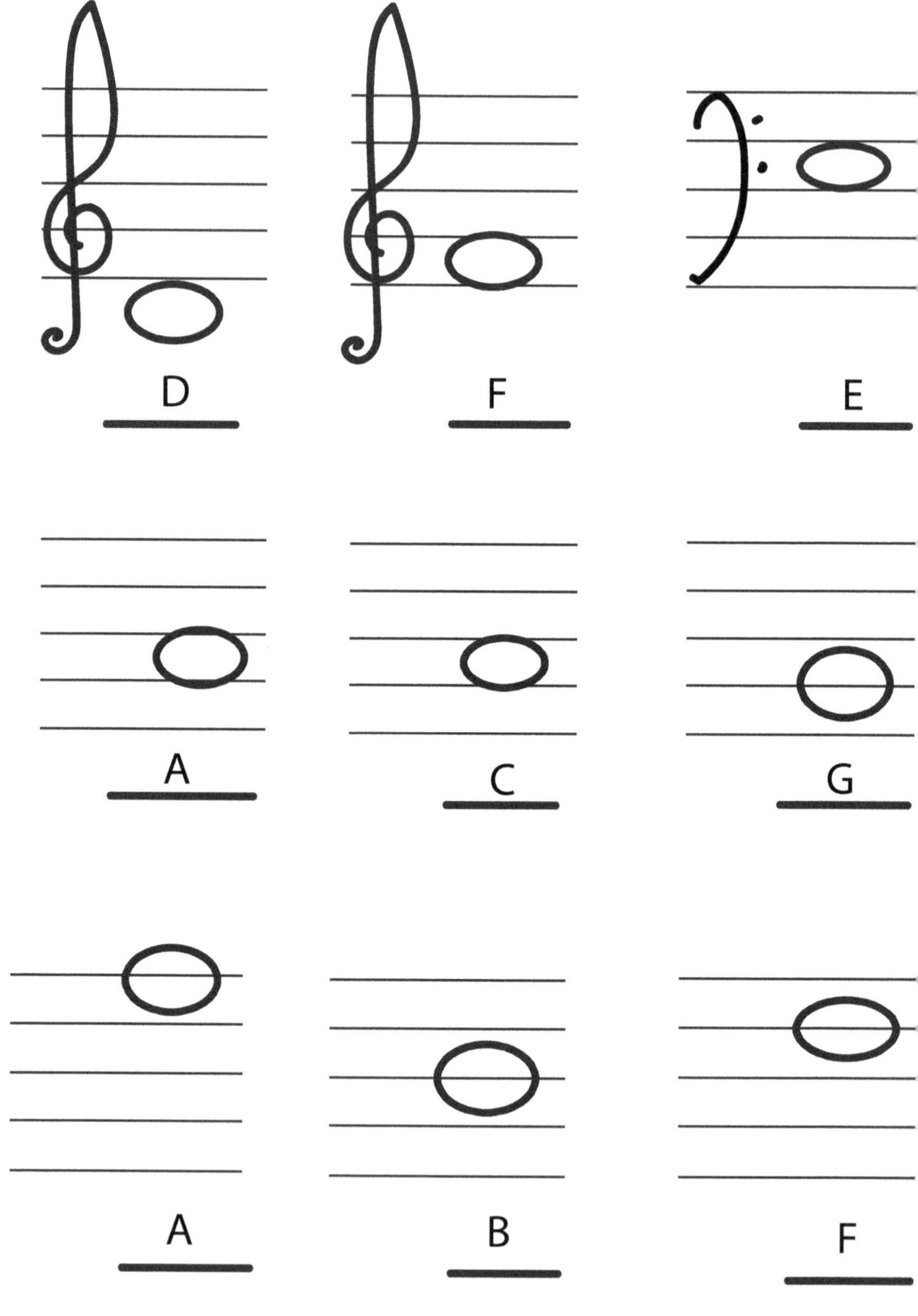

DRAW THE CORRECT CLEF ON STAFF
IS IT BASS CLEF OR TREBLE CLEF?

B

C

B

D

F

D

A

G

E

DRAW THE CORRECT CLEF ON STAFF
IS IT BASS CLEF OR TREBLE CLEF?

F

B

E

G

D

B

F

D

A

RHYTHMS

Name	Note	Rest	Beats
WHOLE			4
HALF			2
QUARTER			1
EIGHTH			1/2
SIXTEENTH			1/4

If you add a dot next to a rhythmic note/rest on the right, the dot adds additional half value of the note/rest. For example, dotted half note would have 1 + 1/2 beats of a half note which would have the same rhythmic sum as having 3 quarter notes. A dotted quarter note would have 1 + 1/2 beats of a quarter note, which would have the same rhythmic sum as having 3 eighth notes. In a rhythmic bar, 4/4 has 4 quarter notes per measure, 3/4 has 3 quarters, 2/4 has 2 quarters per measure & 6/8 has 6 eighth notes per measure. 3 eighths would equal a dotted quarter note and 3 quarters would equal 6 eighth notes in rhythmic sum.

WRITE THE NAMES OF THE DIFFERENT RHYTHMS

DRAW IN THE BAR LINES

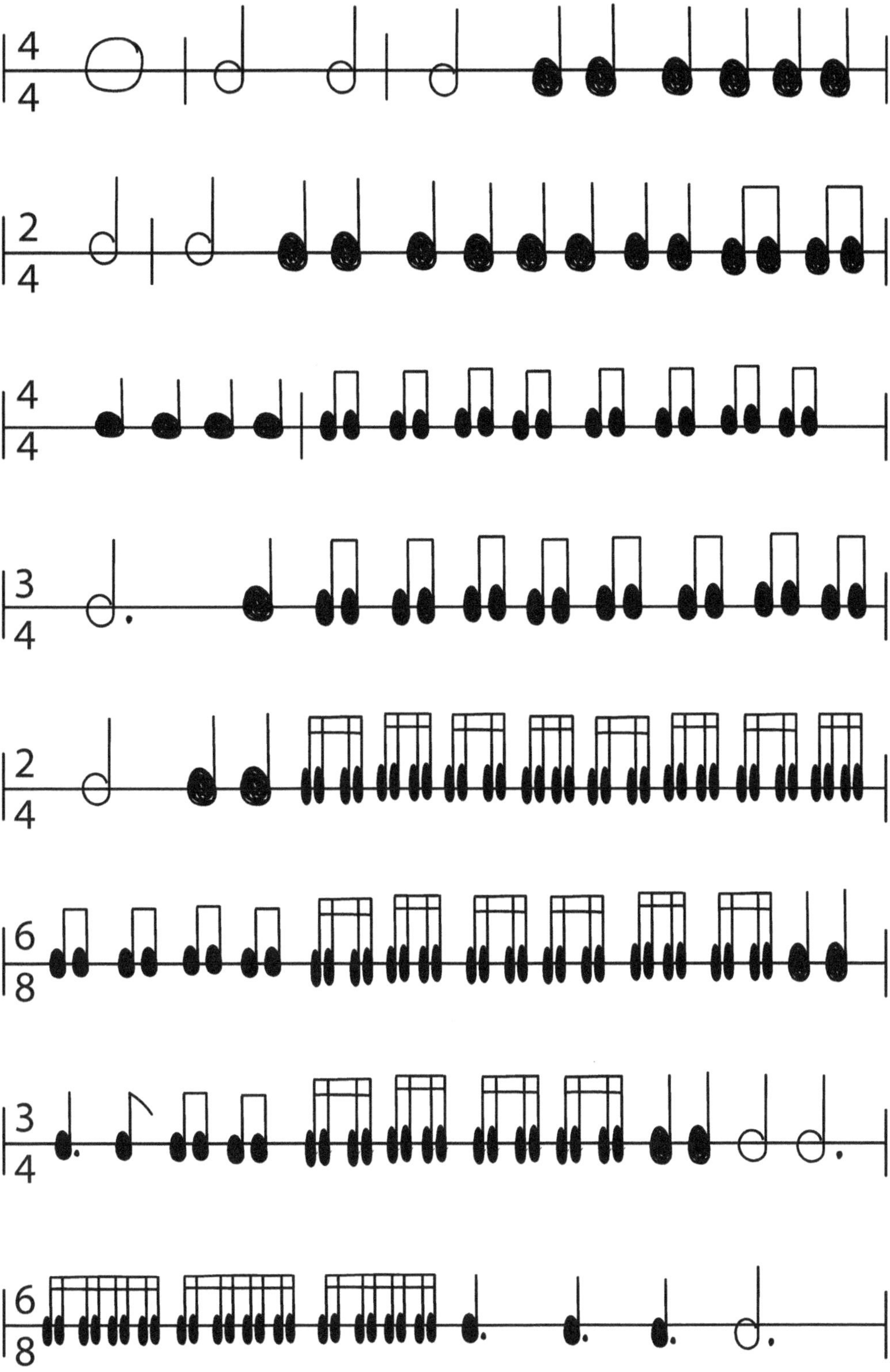

FILL IN THE 4/4 BARS WITH RHYTHMS

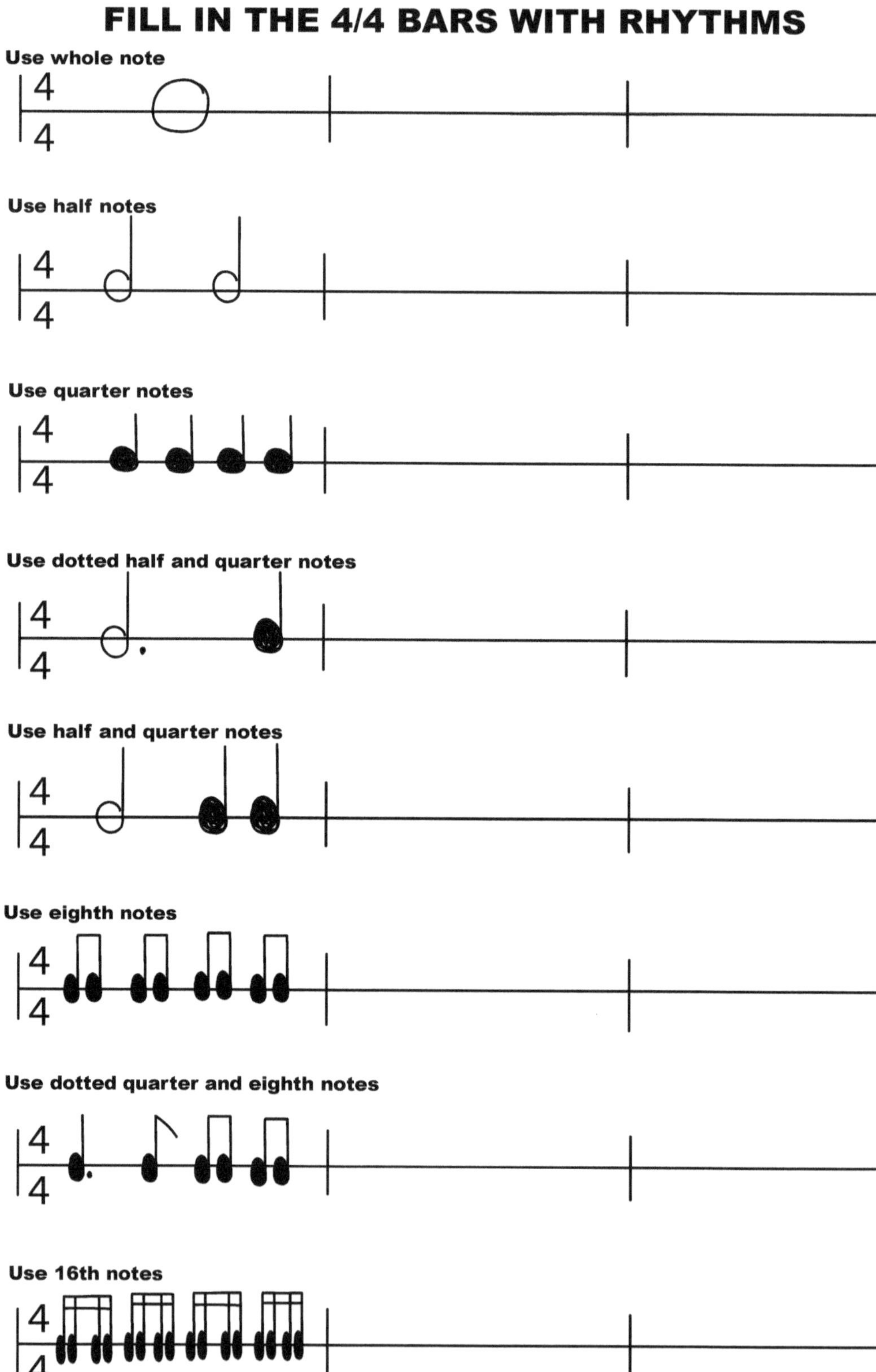

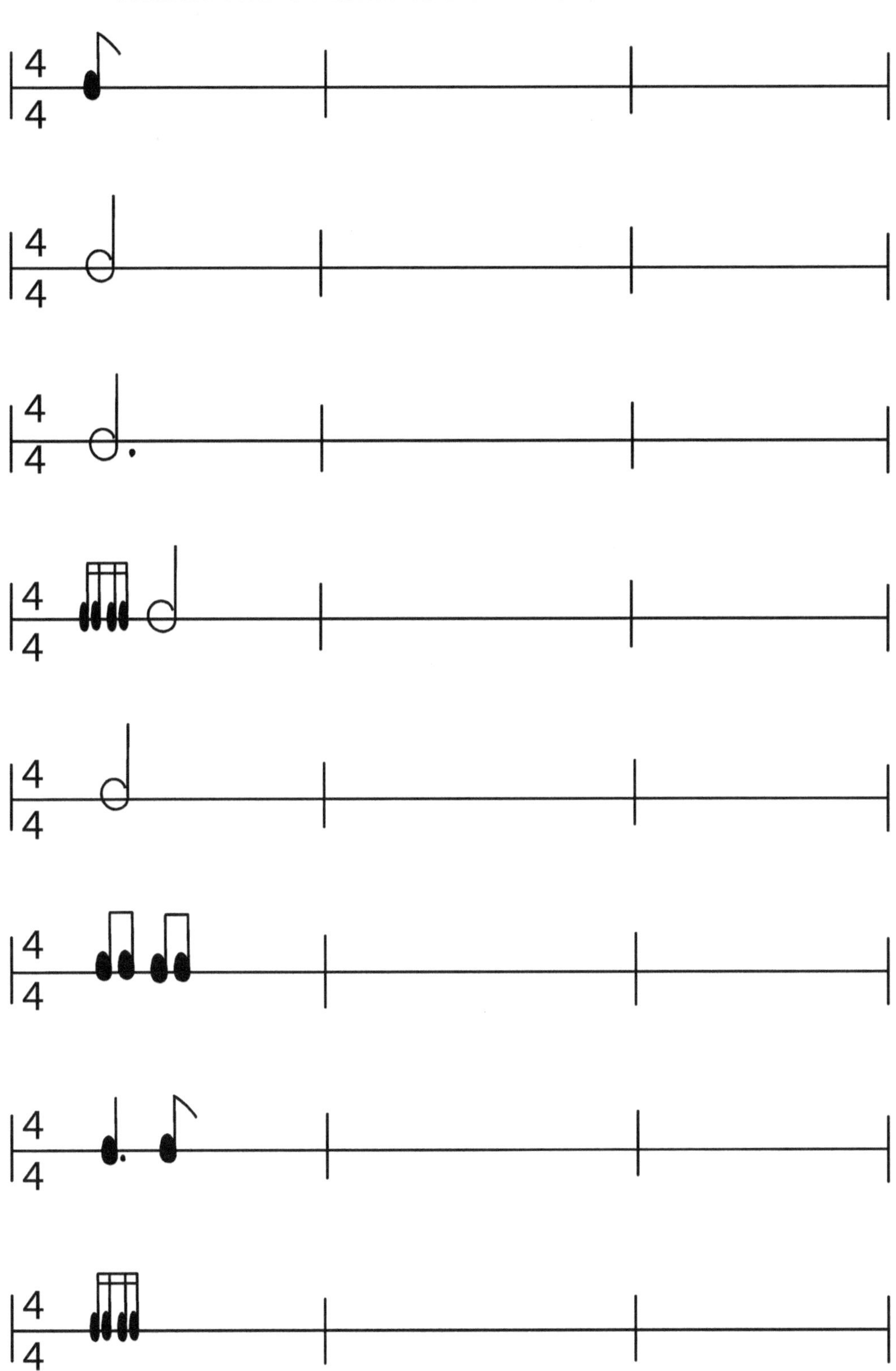

FILL IN THE 4/4 BARS WITH DIFFERENT RHYTHMS

FILL IN THE 3/4 & 2/4 BARS WITH DIFFERENT RHYTHMS

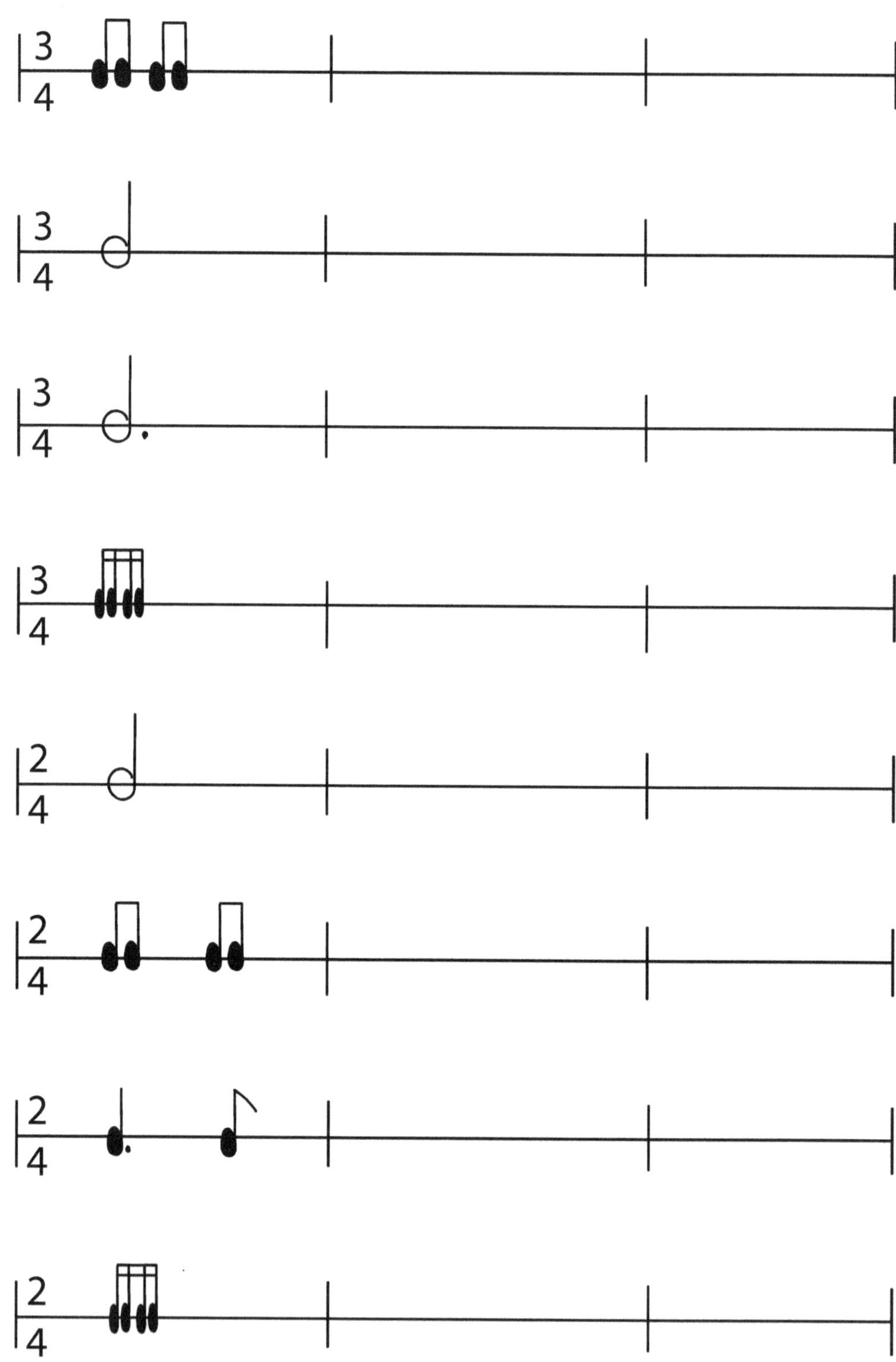

FILL IN THE 6/8 BARS

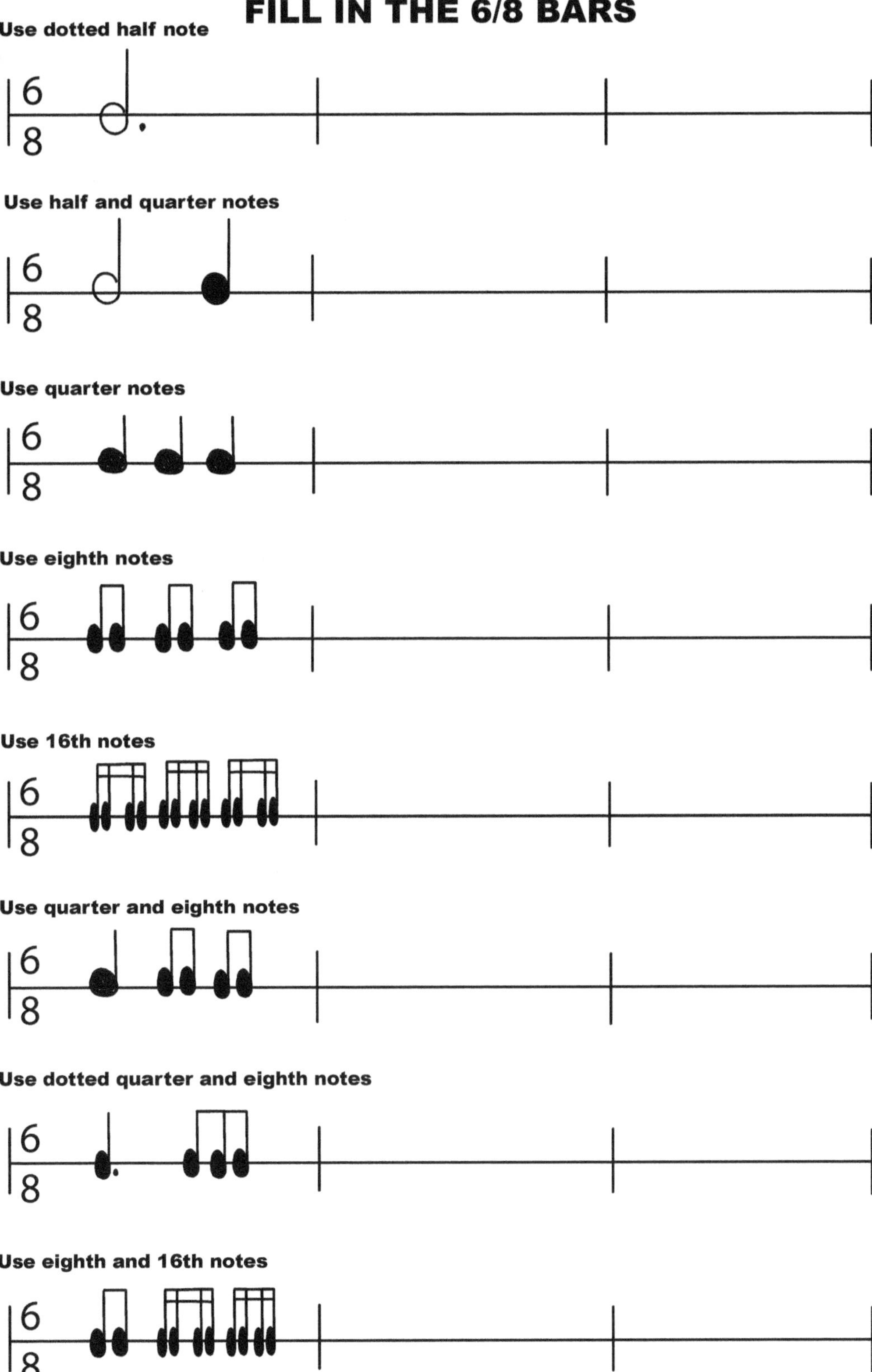

FILL IN THE 6/8 BARS WITH DIFFERENT RHYTHMS

ANSWERS (The notes can be written in different octaves)

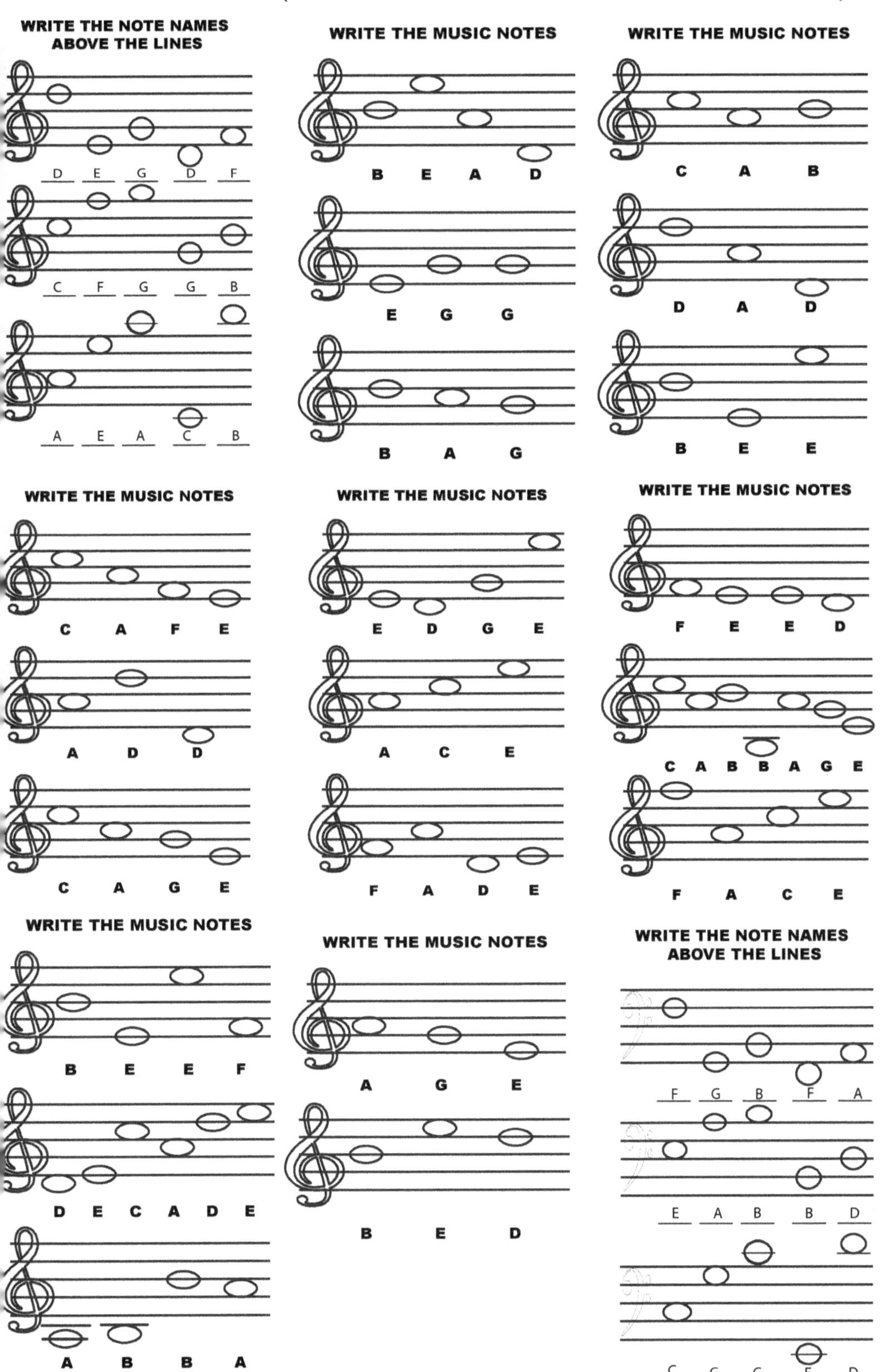

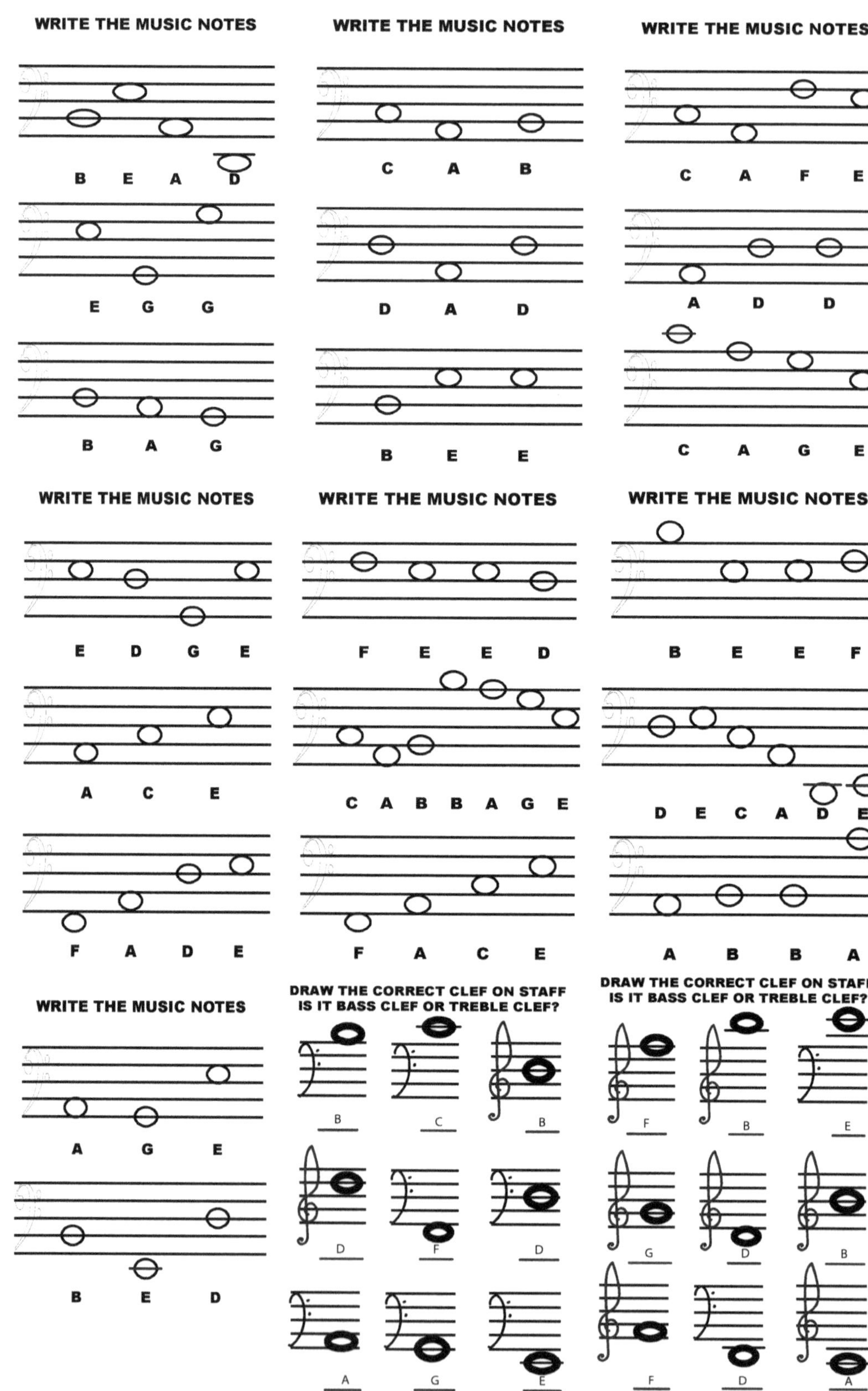
WRITE THE MUSIC NOTES
B E A D
E G G
B A G
WRITE THE MUSIC NOTES
C A B
D A D
B E E
WRITE THE MUSIC NOTES
C A F E
A D D
C A G E
WRITE THE MUSIC NOTES
E D G E
A C E
F A D E
WRITE THE MUSIC NOTES
F E E D
C A B B A G E
F A C E
WRITE THE MUSIC NOTES
B E E F
D E C A D E
A B B A
WRITE THE MUSIC NOTES
A G E
B E D
DRAW THE CORRECT CLEF ON STAFF
IS IT BASS CLEF OR TREBLE CLEF?
B
C
B
D
F
D
A
G
E
DRAW THE CORRECT CLEF ON STAFF
IS IT BASS CLEF OR TREBLE CLEF?
F
B
E
G
D
B
F
D
A

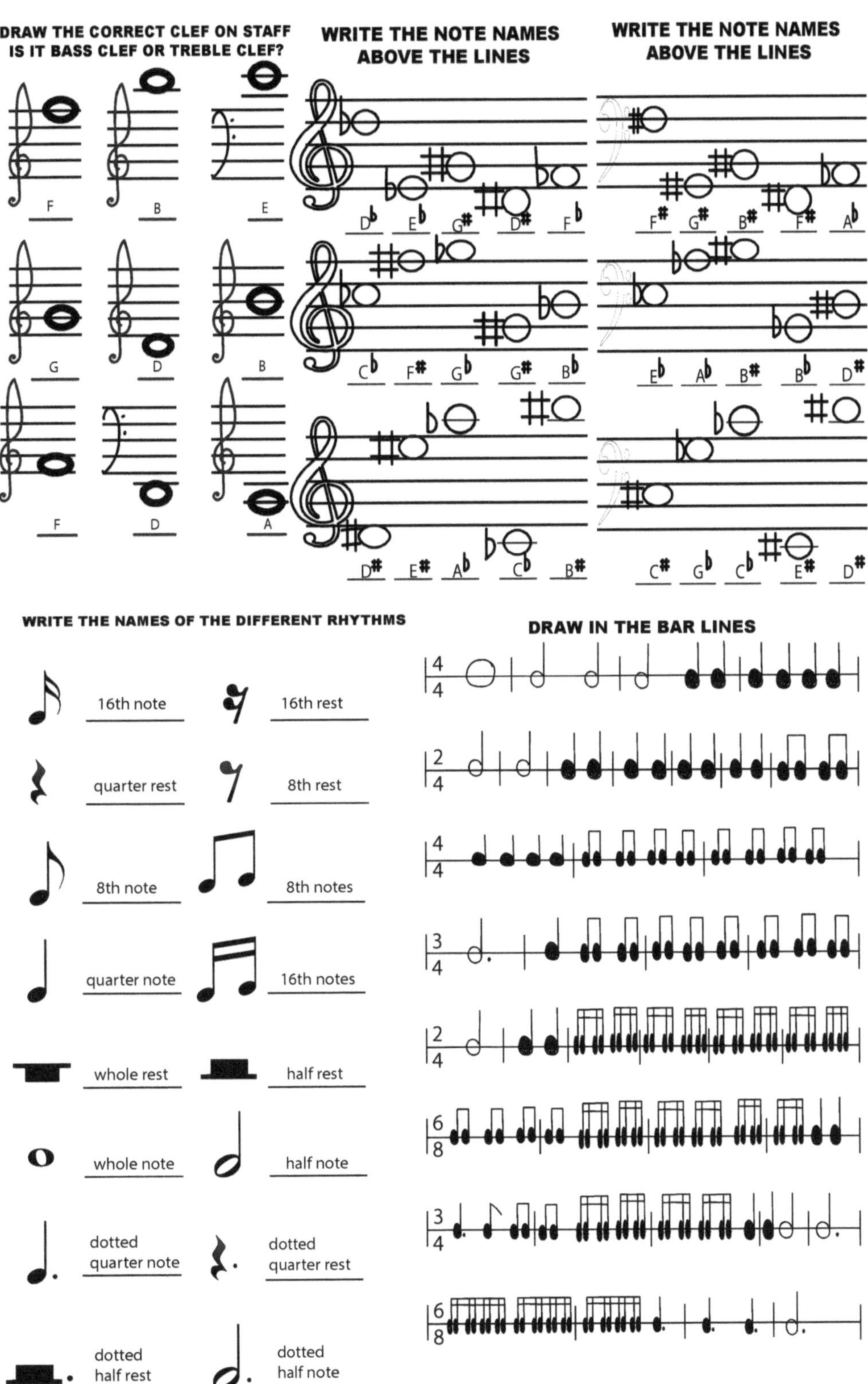

DRAW THE CORRECT CLEF ON STAFF
IS IT BASS CLEF OR TREBLE CLEF?
F
B
E
G
D
B
F
D
A
WRITE THE NOTE NAMES ABOVE THE LINES
Db Eb G# D# Fb
Cb F# Gb G# Bb
D# E# Ab Cb B#
WRITE THE NOTE NAMES ABOVE THE LINES
F# G# B# F# Ab
Eb Ab B# Bb D#
C# Gb Cb E# D#
WRITE THE NAMES OF THE DIFFERENT RHYTHMS
16th note
16th rest
quarter rest
8th rest
8th note
8th notes
quarter note
16th notes
whole rest
half rest
whole note
half note
dotted quarter note
dotted quarter rest
dotted half rest
dotted half note
DRAW IN THE BAR LINES

The names of music notes in English, French, German, Italian, & Spanish

English	French	German	Italian	Spanish
Major	Majeur	Dur	Maggiore	Mayor
Minor	Mineur	Moll	Minore	Menor
Sharp	Dièse	-is	Diesis	Sostenido
Flat	Bémol	-es	Bemolle	Bemol
Note Names				
A flat	La bémol	as	La bemolle	La bemol
A	La	A	La	La
A sharp	La dièse	ais	La diesis	La sostenido
B flat	Si bemol	B	Si bemolle	Si bemol
B	Si	H	Si	Si
C flat	Do bémol	ces	Do bemolle	Do bemol
C	Ut/Do	C	Do	Do
C sharp	Do dièse	cis	Do diesis	Do sostenido
D flat	Ré	des	Re bemolle	Re bemol
D	Ré	D	Re	Re
D sharp	Ré dièse	dis	Re diesis	Re sostenido
E flat	Mi bémol	es	Mi bemolle	Mi bemol
E	Mi	E	Mi	Mi
F	Fa	F	Fa	Fa
F sharp	Fa dièse	fis	Fa diesis	Fa sostenido
G flat	Sol bémol	ges	Sol bemolle	Sol bemol
G	Sol	G	Sol	Sol
G sharp	sol dièse	gis	sol diesis	Sol sostenido

Get the Following Music Theory Books for Students (Varying Difficulty Levels) on Amazon.com

Book 1 Treble Clef
(for ages 3+)
Book also in Spanish, French, German, & Japanese

Book 2 Bass Clef
(for ages 3+)
Book also in Spanish, French, German, & Japanese

Book 3 Treble Clef

Book 4 Bass Clef